AQA AS Accounting
Unit 2 Financial and Management Accounting

By

Brendan Casey

Other Titles in this Series

AQA AS Accounting
Unit 1 Introduction to Financial Accounting

AQA A2 Accounting
Unit 3 Further Aspects of Financial Accounting
Unit 4 Further Aspects of Management Accounting

ISBN 978 1500884266

Table of contents

About the author

The author is Head of Accounting at Ashbourne Independent Sixth Form College in London, and is a graduate of the London School of Economics. He has been teaching the AQA A level accounting syllabus for over 15 years.

Aim of this book

This book is intended as a quick reference revision guide. It's particularly aimed at the written questions, which students often struggle on, but account for about 20-25% of the exam. It also contains appendices of important formats, ratios and definitions.

Types of business organisation

1

1.1 Sole traders

These are businesses where there is only one owner.

Advantages

- Only requires a small amount of capital to start the business
- Owner is working for himself so has an incentive to run the business as efficiently as possible.
- Owner can take decisions quickly because no one else needs to be consulted.
- All profits go to the owner

Disadvantages

- Unlimited liability - this means creditors can claim against the owners personal assets in the event of the business going into liquidation.
- Difficult to obtain extra capital to expand - sole traders seen as being a bigger risk by banks.
- Lack of ideas/creativity - owner working by himself
- Continuity - if owner dies the business dies with him

1.2 Partnerships

This is a business where there are one or more persons joined together in business with a view of making a profit.

Advantages

- More capital – because there is more than owner. It also makes it easier to raise money from banks.
- More ideas - because there is more than one person involved in the business.
- Specialisation can take place - individual partners can adopt different roles, e.g. finance and marketing
- Partners are entitled to a share of profits

Disadvantages

- Unlimited liability
- Disagreements are more likely – because there is more than one owner.
- One partners actions are binding on all the others – this is known as 'joint and several' liability. It means that if one partner makes a mistake, the whole partnership is liable not just the partner who made the mistake.
- Continuity - if one partner dies or leaves a whole new partnership has to start and the partnership agreement has to be drawn up again. This is time consuming.

1.3 Limited company

This is a business where the share capital is split into shares.

Advantages

- Limited liability – this means if the business gets into trouble the creditors can only recover their money against the assets of the business. The personal assets of the owners are safe.
- Easier to raise capital - because they can issue more shares

Disadvantages

- Loss of control – shares can be sold to outsiders so the original owner of the business may lose control of the company.
- Loss of privacy – the accounts of limited companies can be seen by anyone, e.g. competitors.

Accounting principles, concepts and conventions

2

(i) Prudence – this concept states that losses should be recorded as soon as anticipated but profits should only be recorded once realised. Where there is any conflict between the four main concepts (prudence, accruals, consistency and going concern) prudence always takes precedence.

Examples – provision for doubtful debts; inventory is valued at lower of cost and net realisable value.

(ii) Accruals – this concept states that costs and revenues should be matched against one another as far as possible. This means that revenues and expenses are recorded on an earned or incurred basis not receipts and payments. It's also known as the matching concept.

Examples – depreciation; accruals and prepayments.

(iii) Consistency – this concept states that items should be given the same accounting treatment from one year to the next. Firms can still change the accounting treatment if they think it gives a truer and fairer view but they must put a note to the accounts showing the effect and the reason for the change. The consistency concept ensures that the accounts are comparable from one year to the next.

Examples – depreciation; inventory valuation

(iv) Going concern – this concept states that the business should be viewed as a 'going concern'. This means that it is assumed the business will continue for the foreseeable future. The major consequence of this is that assets are valued at cost not what they would fetch if you sell them. As a 'going concern' the assumption is the business will need the assets, and not just treat them as if the business is about to close down and get the best price they can.

Examples – non-current assets are valued at cost.

(v) Cost – this concept states that assets should be valued at cost. This is because cost is an objective measure not a matter of opinion. Therefore it's safer and more prudent.

Examples – non-current assets are valued at cost.

(vi) Materiality – this concept states that the accounts should focus on matters of significance not on the trivial or unimportant.

Examples

- Calculators, staplers and rulers are classified as office expenses not non-current assets even though strictly speaking they are. This is because the amounts involved aren't significant.
- If a firm has already prepared its final accounts and suddenly finds an invoice for £250 it wouldn't be expected to prepare the accounts all over again.

(vii) Objectivity – this concept states that accountants should draw up the accounts on the basis of the guidelines given by the profession, e.g. SSAP's, FRS's, IAS's. They shouldn't just use their own personal opinions.

Examples – inventory valuation; depreciation.

(viii) Realisation – this concept states that revenue should only be recorded once delivery has been made to a customer's firm order.

Example - unsold inventory bought on a 'sales or return' basis remains the property of the seller even though it may be on the buyer's premises.

(ix) Business entity – this concept states that the accounts should only record the financial transactions of the business. The owner's personal financial transactions are a separate matter.

Example – if the owner buys a car for himself using his own money this is a personal transaction and has nothing to do with the business.

Bad debts recovered and provision for doubtful debts

3

3.1 Bad debts recovered

These are bad debts that have previously been written off but are then unexpectedly recovered.

Double-entry

(i) Put cash received in bank and credit bad debts recovered

Dr. Bank
Cr. Bad debts recovered

(ii) Transfer bad debt recovered to income statement

Dr. Bad debts recovered
Cr. Income statement

(iv) Overall effect

	Profit	Cash/Bank
Bad debt recovered	+	+

3.2 Provision for doubtful debts

This is an amount set aside against profits to provide for debts that you think may not be recoverable. Usually it's expressed as a percentage of the final value of the trade receivables, e.g. 5%, 3%.

Double-entry

Dr. Income statement
Cr. Provision for doubtful debts

3.3 Factors used to determine the size of the provision for doubtful debts

Past experience – firms can use their past experience as to the collectability of debts.

Age of trade receivables – the older the debts the more likely they won't be collectable. An aged trade receivable listing is useful here.

Economic cycle – if the economy is in recession you would expect firms to raise their provision.

Geography – if many of the trade receivables are known to be in a region which is in recession you would expect a firm to raise its provision.

3.4 Methods of controlling and managing trade receivables

Aged trade receivable listing – this is a breakdown of trade receivables into bands of thirty days, i.e. 30 days, 60 days, 90 days, and 120 days. From this an accountant can monitor the debts of the company and take action where necessary.

Cash discounts for prompt payment – this creates an incentive to pay quickly and should reduce trade receivables building up.

Chase trade receivables regularly – send out trade receivable statements every month and follow up troublesome trade receivables with a phone call.

Set credit limits – give all clients a credit limit so they can't run up large debts.

Check credit references – use a credit agency to determine the credit worthiness of new clients before giving them an account.

3.5 Why is it necessary to make a provision for doubtful debts?

It's necessary to make a provision for doubtful debts because of the prudence concept. This states that losses should be provided for once anticipated, but profits should only be recorded once realised. On this basis if there is any doubt that all the debts won't be collected then a firm must make a provision for doubtful debts. Otherwise the accounts will fail to reflect a 'true and fair view'.

Income received in advance and due

4

4.1 Income received in advance

Examples

- Rent received in advance from a tenant
- Commission received in advance from a client.

It's a current liability because technically at the year end this money still belongs to what is normally a "other receivable" (see below). Its classified as "other payables"

'T 'account

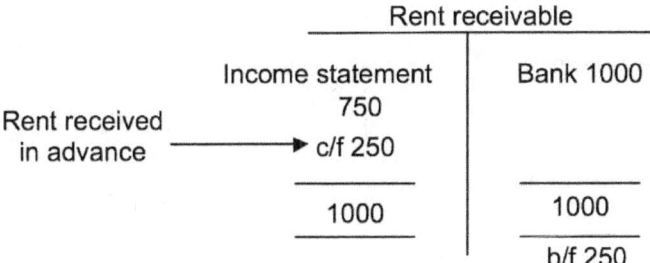

Rent receivable

Income statement 750	Bank 1000
Rent received in advance → c/f 250	
1000	1000
	b/f 250

4.2 Income due

Examples

- Interest due
- Rent due

It's a current asset at the year end because money is due from a debtor. Its classified as "other receivables".

'T' account

Income received in advance and due

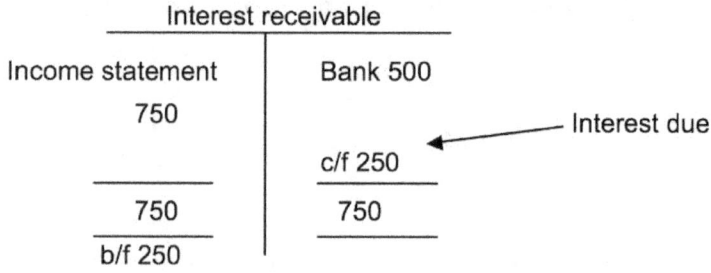

Interest receivable

Income statement 750	Bank 500
	c/f 250 — Interest due
750	750
b/f 250	

4.3 'T' account entries - this year's/last year's accruals/prepayments

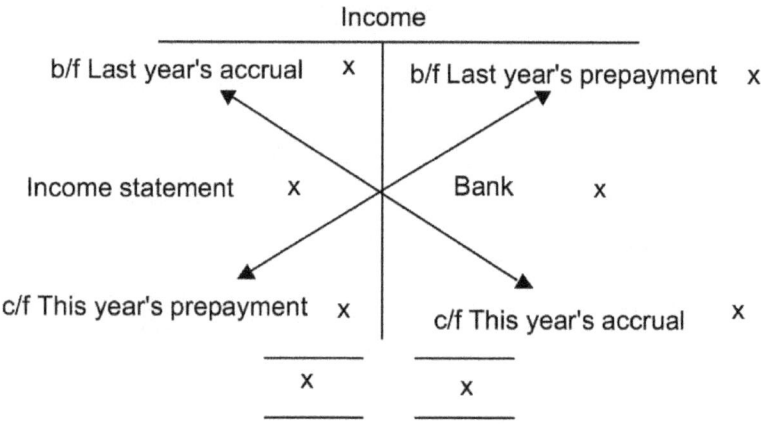

Income

b/f Last year's accrual X	b/f Last year's prepayment X
Income statement X	Bank X
c/f This year's prepayment X	c/f This year's accrual X
X	X

The T account entries for last year's accruals/prepayments work exactly the same way as for expense accounts; you find them *diagonally opposite* this year's accruals/prepayments. Notice that in an income account all the entries are on the opposite side for what you would find in an expense account. If you want to memorise the T account above, my advice would be to be very sure about the position of one of the figures, e.g. this year's accrued income, and the other three will automatically follow.

Depreciation

5

5.1 Definition

Long definition - depreciation is a measure of the wearing out, consumption or other loss of value of a non-current asset whether due to use, time or obsolescence through technological innovation or market change.

Short definition – the apportioning of the cost of a non-current asset over its estimated useful economic life.

5.2 Causes of depreciation

We can see the causes of depreciation by looking at the long definition:

- Wear and tear
- Time
- Technological improvement
- Market change

5.3 Methods

(i) Straight line

This means charging the same amount of depreciation for a non-current asset every year. It should be used where a non-current asset is going to be used evenly over its useful life, e.g. fixtures and fittings.

Formula

$$\text{Straight line} = \frac{(\text{Cost} - \text{residual value})}{\text{Estimated useful life in years}}$$

(ii) Reducing balance

This means charging a higher amount of depreciation in the early years than in the later years. It should be used when an asset is going to be more heavily used at the beginning of its life than at the end, e.g. plant & machinery, motor cars.

Formula

Reducing balance = NBV at previous balance sheet date x percentage rate

5.4 Double entry

Dr. Income statement
Cr. Provision for depreciation

5.5 Objectives/purposes

To satisfy the accruals concept – the accruals concept says that costs have to be matched against revenues as far as possible. Therefore we need to spread the cost of the non-current asset over its useful life and charge it to several accounting periods not just charge the whole cost in the year of purchase.
To ensure balance sheet values for non-current assets are fairly stated – if depreciation was not charged then the non-current asset values would remain at cost. This would mean the accounts would fail to reflect a true and fair view.
It may retain funds in the business for the replacement of non-current assets – depreciation reduces the amount of profit available for dividends or drawings. This helps retain funds in the business which may be used for the replacement of non-current assets.

5.6 Disposal of non-current assets

You can calculate the gain or loss on disposal of a non-current asset using either a formula or a disposals account.

Formula

Gain/loss on disposal = sale proceeds – net book value

Disposals account

Depreciation

Disposal

Cost 10,000	Provn for depn 5,000
Income statement (Gain) 1,000	Bank 6,000
11,000	11,000

5.7 Effect of depreciation on cash flow

Depreciation has no effect on cash flow because it's a non-cash expense. It reduces profit but not cash.

Capital/revenue expenditure, capital/revenue income

6

6.1 Definitions

Capital expenditure – this means spending on non-current assets or improving non-current assets, e.g. plant & machinery, motor cars. It includes any transportation or installation costs associated with the asset.
Revenue expenditure – this means spending on the day-to-day running costs of the business, e.g. rent, light & heat.
Capital income – this means money coming into the business either from new capital or the disposal of non-current assets, e.g. issue of shares, disposal of property.
Revenue income – this means income from the normal trading activities of the business, e.g. sales.

6.2 Why is it important to distinguish between capital and revenue expenditure?

To ensure profits are fairly stated – if revenue expenditure was wrongly classified as capital expenditure this would mean profits would be overstated. If capital expenditure was wrongly classified as revenue expenditure this would mean profits would be understated.
To ensure non-current assets are correctly valued on the balance sheet – if revenue expenditure was wrongly classified as capital expenditure then non-current assets would be overstated. If capital expenditure was wrongly classified as revenue expenditure then non-current assets would be understated. Therefore the balance sheet would fail to show a true and fair view.

Inventory valuation

7

The general rule is that inventory is valued at the lower of cost and net realisable value (NRV). Net realisable value is the selling price of the goods minus the costs of getting it into a saleable condition. This includes marketing costs, commission and repair costs. In questions the focus tends to be on how to value damaged inventory.

Example

Items	Cost	Selling price	Cost of getting goods into a saleable condition	NRV	Inventory valuation
A	500	600	50	550	500
B	100	150	60	90	90
C	1000	1200	100	1100	1000

Replacement cost

If you ever see replacement cost in questions ignore it. It's not used in UK accounting.

Limited companies

8

8.1 Definition

Limited companies are companies whose capital is split into shares. There are two types:

Private limited companies - these are companies whose shares are not available to the general public and are not available on the stock market. They have the letters 'Ltd' after their name, e.g. Virgin Ltd.
Public limited company – these are companies whose shares are available to the general public and are available on the stock market. They must have a share capital of at least £50,000. They have the letters 'plc' after their name, e.g. Marks & Spencer plc.

8.2 Ownership and control

The shareholders own the company, the directors run it on their behalf. In smaller limited companies the directors may have substantial shareholdings but in large plc's their shareholding is usually nominal. Every year there is an Annual General Meeting where the shareholders can re-appoint or not re-appoint the directors. There is said to be a 'divorce between ownership and control'.

8.3 Limited liability

This is one of the main benefits of forming a limited company. It means that if the business gets into trouble the creditors can only recover their money against the assets the business. The personal assets of the shareholders are safe.

8.4 Layouts

For the purposes of the exam you only need to know the layout of the internal financial accounts of limited companies. See Appendices 3 and 4 for examples of income statements (trading and profit and loss account) and balance sheets (statement of financial position).

8.5 Authorised share capital, issued share capital and called-up share capital

Authorised share capital – this is the amount of share capital a company can issue if it wants to.
Issued share capital - this is the amount of share capital a company has actually issued. **Called-up share capital** - this is the amount of share capital which has been paid for when shares have been issued partly paid, e.g. if 100,000 £1 shares were issued partly paid at 40p then £40,000 is the "called up" share capital and £60,000 is the "uncalled" share capital. Only the called-up share capital can be shown on the balance sheet.

In terms of calculations of dividends the dividend is based on the issued or called-up share capital. You can ignore the authorised share capital.

8.6 Ordinary (equity) shares

(i) Definition

Ordinary (equity) shares represent part ownership in a limited company. They are the most widely available form of shares and are also referred to as equity capital.

(ii) Features

- Variable dividend – ordinary (equity) shareholders are entitled to a dividend every year.
- Voting rights – each share carries one vote and gives shareholders the right to appoint/re-appoint directors.

(iii) Advantages/disadvantages from shareholder's point of view

Advantages

- Higher returns – ordinary (equity) shareholders can get a return from two sources. An income gain from the dividend and a capital gain from an increase in the share price.
- Voting rights - voting rights give ordinary (equity) shareholders a certain amount control over how the business is run.

Disadvantages

- More risk - if the company goes into liquidation the ordinary (equity) shareholders are the last group of people to receive any

return after all the other creditors have been paid, e.g. trade payables, banks, debenture holders, preference shareholders.
- May get no dividend - the directors don't have to pay the ordinary (equity) shareholders any dividend if they don't want to.
- Receive their dividend after preference shareholders have been paid.

(iv) Advantages/disadvantages from firm's point of view

Advantages

- Variable dividend – if profits are low firm doesn't have to pay a dividend. This is good for cash flow and liquidity.
- Dividend not carried forward from one year to the next – unlike preference shares.
- Don't have to repay capital – unlike bank loans

Disadvantages

- Voting rights – can be a problem if shareholders are dissatisfied with company performance.
- Takes longer to raise capital – unlike bank loans which by comparison are easier to arrange.

8.7 Preference shares

(i) Definition

Preference shares also represent part ownership in a limited company. They are less widely available than ordinary shares.

(ii) Features

- Fixed dividend - preference shares pay a fixed dividend every year.
- No voting rights - preference shareholders have no voting rights.

(iii) Advantages/disadvantages from shareholder's point of view

Advantages

- Greater security/less risk - preference shareholders are entitled to a fixed dividend every year and the share price fluctuates much less than ordinary (equity) shares.
- Rank before ordinary shareholders in case of liquidation.
- Receive dividend before ordinary (equity) shareholders.

Disadvantages

- No voting rights - preference shareholders can't influence the way the company is run.
- Lower returns - preference shares are less risky and so the share price won't go up as much as that of ordinary (equity) shares. The main form of return is just the dividend.

(iv) Advantages/disadvantages from firm's point of view

Advantages

- Fixed dividend – so if firm has made good profits more profit can be retained in the business.
- No vote – so less disruptive from a director's point of view.

Disadvantages

- Fixed dividend – dividend still has to be paid even if the firm has had a bad year.
- Dividend usually cumulative – it carries forward from one year to the next even if there wasn't enough money to pay for it. See (v) below.
- May be redeemable – see (v) below.

(v) Other types of preference shares

Redeemable cumulative preference shares - these type of preference shares can be redeemed (i.e. paid back) by the company at any time and the dividend is carried forward from one year to the next. This means that if in one year the company doesn't have enough profit to pay its preference dividend it's automatically carried forward to the next accounting period and the company still has to pay it. This continues into succeeding accounting periods.

Irredeemable non-cumulative preference shares - this type of preference share can't be redeemed by the company and the dividend can't be carried forward by the shareholders from one accounting period to the next. This means that if in one year the company doesn't have enough profit to pay its preference dividend the preference shareholders lose it.

8.8 Debentures

(i) Definition

Debentures are fixed interest loans secured against non-current assets repayable at a set date. The security is usually land & buildings. If the company defaults on the loan the debenture holders can take possession of the security and sell it to settle their debt.

(ii) Example

6% Debenture 2018 - £250,000

This means the amount of the loan is £250,000, the interest rate is 6% and the repayment date is 2018.

(iii) Features

- Fixed interest payments
- Long-term loan with security

(iv) Advantages/disadvantages from debenture holder's point of view

Advantages

- Fixed return - debenture holders know they will get a fixed return each year
- Lower risk - in case of the company defaulting on its debt or going into liquidation the debenture holders can take possession of their security and sell it.

Disadvantages

- Lower returns - the return is fixed to the level of the interest rate.
- No voting rights - debenture holders have no voting rights so they can't influence the company in any way.

8.9 Share premium account

Limited companies

The share premium account arises when shares are issued at a price above their nominal value (face value). The difference between the nominal value and the issue price goes into a share premium account.

Example

XYZ plc issues 100,000 £1 ordinary shares at £1.50 in order to raise more capital for expansion.

Double-entry

Dr. Bank	£150,000	
Cr. Ordinary (equity) shares		£100,000
Cr. Share Premium Account		£50,000

8.10 Revaluation reserve

A revaluation reserve arises when the property of a company is revalued upwards at the end of the year. The difference between the original and new values goes into a revaluation reserve.

Example

XYZ Ltd revalues its land & buildings from £1m to £1.2m at the end of the year.

Double-entry

Dr. Land & buildings	£200,000	
Cr. Revaluation reserve		£200,000

8.11 Calculation of dividends

(i) Formulas

- Ordinary (equity) share dividend = Number of shares x dividend per share
- Preference share dividend = Value of shares x preference share percentage

Where:

$$\text{Number of shares} = \frac{\text{Total value of shares}}{\text{Nominal value per share}}$$

(ii) Example

XYZ Ltd has the following share capital:

50p Ordinary (equity) shares = £500,000
6% £1 Preference shares = £100,000

Calculate its ordinary (equity) share dividend and preference share dividend for the year if the ordinary (equity) share dividend is 8p per share.

Solution

- Ordinary (equity) dividend = (£500,000 ÷ 50p) x 8p = £80,000
- Preference dividend = £100,000 x 6% = £6,000

(iii) Ordinary (equity) share dividend expressed as a percentage

Calculate these exactly the same way as preference share dividends. Mostly though the examiner will express ordinary (equity) share dividends in pence and preference share dividends as a percentage.

8.12 Treatment of dividends in financial statements

Because of IAS 1 the appropriation account has been more or less replaced by the statement of changes in equity. The new treatment of dividends is now as follows:

- Ordinary (equity) dividends paid during year – included in statement of changes in equity.
- Preference dividends paid during year – included in "finance costs" in Income Statement.
- Ordinary (equity) dividends proposed at end of year – disclosed by way of note to the accounts.

For statement of changes in equity see 8.16 below. IAS's and notes to the accounts are covered in Unit 3.

8.13 Capital reserves & revenue reserves

Limited companies

The reserves section on the balance sheet contains two types of reserves - capital reserves and revenue reserves. By convention you should always show the capital reserves first.

Revenue reserves - these are reserves which have been created from surplus profits. They can be used for distribution of dividends and also for capital purposes, e.g. issue of bonus shares.

Examples: Retained profits, general reserve.

Capital reserves - these are reserves which have not been created from surplus profits. They are not available for distribution of dividends and can only be used for capital purposes, e.g. bonus issues.

Examples: Share premium account, revaluation reserve.

8.14 Operating profit, interim dividends, loan capital and shareholders' funds

Operating profit - this means the profit on the businesses normal trading activities. It's defined as profit before tax and interest. See appendix 3.

Interim dividend - this is a dividend which is paid 6 months into the financial year.

Final dividend – this is the dividend proposed by directors at the end of the year subject to approval by the shareholders at the Annual General Meeting (AGM).

Loan capital - this is the medium to long-term capital of a limited company provided either by banks or debenture holders.

Shareholders' funds - this is all of the share capital of the company plus all reserves. It includes both ordinary and preference shares.

8.15 Rights issues and bonus issues

(i) Rights issue

This is an offer of shares for cash to existing shareholders. The shareholders can either take up the offer or sell their rights to a third party, hence the name. The shares can be issued at either par or a premium.

Purpose

The purpose of a rights issue is to raise finance.

<u>Advantages as a source of finance</u>

- No interest to pay – unlike a bank loan or debenture
- Don't have to pay the money back – again unlike a bank loan or debenture
- Don't need to offer any security – therefore does not put the firm at risk
- Creates a sense of loyalty amongst the shareholders – because they are making a bigger financial commitment.

<u>Advantages over an issue of shares to the general public</u>

- It's cheaper – share issues on the stock market are expensive because merchant banks and lawyers have to be paid.
- It's got a better chance of success – because you are approaching your own shareholders who know the company better.

<u>Double-Entry</u>

Dr. Bank
Cr. Ordinary (equity) share capital
Cr. Share premium

<u>(ii) Bonus issues</u>

This is a free issue of shares to existing shareholders. The shares are paid for out of existing reserves. The reserves used may be capital or revenue reserves. It's also known as a scrip issue.

<u>Advantage from shareholders point of view</u>

- Shareholders get more shares – therefore increases the value of their shareholding assuming the share price doesn't fall in proportion to the number of shares issued.
- Provided the rate of dividend is maintained it increases their dividends in the future as well.
- Lowers the share price – therefore makes the shares more marketable.

<u>Advantage from company/directors point of view</u>

- Rewards the shareholders without using any cash – it therefore protects the working capital of the business.
- It helps to foster loyalty amongst the shareholders who feel rewarded.

<u>Double-Entry</u>

Dr. Reserves (question will specify)
Cr. Ordinary (equity) share capital

<u>8.16 Statement of changes in equity</u>

This summarises the movements in the equity section of the balance sheet during the year. See Appendix 5 for layout. Notice that it includes these important items:

- Shares issued during the year – includes rights issues and bonus issues
- Profit for year
- Ordinary (equity) dividends paid during year – this would normally be this year's interim dividend and last year's final.
- Revaluation of property – revaluation reserve

Preference share dividends are now included under "finance costs" in the Income Statement. The final proposed ordinary (equity) share dividend is disclosed by way of note to the accounts.

<u>8.17 Evaluation of issue of shares and loan capital as sources of finance</u>

When comparing these methods of raising finance bear in mind the following points:

Dilution of control - issuing shares may mean diluting control of the company but issuing debentures or taking on a bank loan won't.
Interest – issuing debentures or taking on bank loans will increase interest payments. Issuing shares is 'free'.
How quickly the company needs the money – arranging a bank loan will probably be a lot quicker and cheaper than issuing shares or debentures. These require the specialist skills of merchant banks and lawyers so will take time and cost money.
Repayment – shares don't have to be repaid, loans and debentures do.

Security - debentures and bank loans require security from the lender. If the firm can't keep up with the payments it may put the business at risk.

Ratio analysis and the assessment of business performance

9

The purpose of ratio analysis is to analyse the accounts and give them some meaning. There are four types you need to know for the unit.

- Performance ratios
- Activity ratios
- Liquidity ratios
- Gearing ratio

9.1 Performance ratios

(i) Return on capital employed (ROCE)

Formula

$$ROCE = \frac{\text{Profit before tax \& interest (operating profit)}}{\text{Debentures} + \text{long term bank loans} + \text{share capital} + \text{reserves}} \times 100$$

Meaning

It shows shareholders the return on the money they have invested in the business. If we imagine profit on capital is like interest for a person with a savings account then shareholders will want to make at least what they could make by just leaving their money in the bank, e.g. 5%.

Reasons for it increasing

- Better use of asset base

Reasons for it decreasing

- Worse use of asset base

(ii) Gross profit margin

Formula

$$\text{Gross Profit Margin} = \frac{\text{Gross profit}}{\text{Revenue}} \times 100$$

Meaning

It shows the difference between the buying price(s) and selling price(s) as a percentage of sales. It can be improved by either purchasing cheaper goods or by increasing the selling price to customers.

Reasons for it decreasing

- Greater competition – therefore had to decrease selling prices
- Higher prices from suppliers

Reasons for it increasing

- Weaker competition – therefore able to increase prices
- New successful products – therefore able to increase prices
- Cheaper prices from suppliers

(iii) Profit in relation to revenue

Formula

$$\text{Profit in relation to revenue} = \frac{\text{Profit for year}}{\text{Revenue}} \times 100$$

Meaning

It shows profit for the year as a percentage of sales. It shows how well a business is controlling its overheads.

Reasons for it increasing

- Firm is getting better at controlling its overheads
- Gross profit has increased – therefore there's a knock-on effect to profit in relation to revenue

Reason for it decreasing

- Firm is getting worse at controlling its overheads

- Gross profit has decreased – therefore there's a knock-on effect to profit in relation to revenue

(iv) Mark-up

Formula

$$Mark-up = \frac{Gross\ profit}{Cost\ of\ sales} \times 100$$

Meaning

Mark-up shows a business's gross profit as a percentage of cost of sales. It can be improved by either purchasing cheaper goods or by increasing the selling price to customers.

(v) Overheads revenue percentage

Formula

$$Overheads\ revenue\ percentage = \frac{Overheads}{Revenue} \times 100$$

Meaning

It measures a firm's overheads as a percentage of sales. It shows their ability to control their overheads. To improve the percentage the firm must either reduce expenses or increase the selling price to customers.

9.2 Activity ratios

(i) Inventory turnover ratio

Formula

$$Inventory\ turnover = \frac{Cost\ of\ sales}{Average\ inventory}$$

Or

$$\text{Inventory turnover} = \frac{\text{Average inventory}}{\text{Cost of sales}} \times 365 \text{ days}$$

Where

$$\text{Average inventory} = \frac{1}{2} \times (\text{opening inventory} + \text{closing inventory})$$

Meaning

It shows how quickly inventory is moving through the firm from delivery to sale. If it's moving more slowly than other firms that are comparable this means liquidity will suffer because more cash will be tied up in inventory.

(ii) Receivable days

Formula

$$\text{Receivable days} = \frac{\text{Trade receivables}}{\text{Credit sales}} \times 365 \text{ days}$$

Meaning

It shows how long it takes a firm to collect its debts. A good figure is about 30 days, anything over 90 days and the business is having problems. Businesses will usually put up with 30-60 days because they don't want to damage customer relations.

Problem of having a high receivable days period

- Weakens cash flow – the firm will have less money to pay off its short-term liabilities, e.g. suppliers and expenses.
- Bad debts – there is a greater risk of bad debts and therefore it effects profits.

How to solve a receivable days problem

- Offer cash discounts for prompt payment, e.g. 5% off if debt is settled in 10 days.

- Tighten up administration system, e.g. chase trade receivables by telephoning or sending reminder letters; send out monthly statements.
- Set credit limits for trade receivables - review credit facilities regularly; suspend account if necessary

(iii) Payable days

Formula

$$\text{Payable days} = \frac{\text{Trade payables}}{\text{Credit purchases}} \times 365 \text{ days}$$

Meaning

It measures the amount of time it takes a business to pay its trade payables. Generally the longer it takes the better as it improves the business's liquidity. However, care must be taken not to annoy suppliers as they may refuse to supply goods if the firm takes too long.

9.3 Liquidity ratios

(i) Net current asset ratio

It's also sometimes called the working capital ratio.

Formula

$$\text{Net current asset ratio} = \frac{\text{Current assets}}{\text{Current liabilities}}$$

Usefulness

It measures how easily a business can meet its short-term liabilities. The ideal figure is between I.5 - 2.

Problems of excessive working capital

- Too much money tied up in unproductive assets - e.g. inventory, bank. This money could be put to better use.
- Puts off potential investors - makes the business look as if it isn't well managed.

Problems of limited working capital

- May not be able to take advantage of business opportunities as they come along - not enough cash available.
- May place business at risk from liquidation.

Ways of increasing working capital

- Issue of shares, e.g. rights issue
- Issue of debentures
- Bank loan
- Sell surplus non-current assets
- Reduce dividend payments
- Cut costs
- Sell surplus inventory

Evaluative points to consider if asked to choose the most suitable way a business could increase their working capital

- Costs - e.g. bank loan (interest) vs. issue of shares (no interest)
- Control – e.g. issue of shares (dilution of control) vs. debentures (no dilution of control)
- Time - e.g. bank loan (a month) vs. issue of shares (6-12 months)

Ways of controlling working capital in a business

- Prepare cash budgets - this will give an idea of what the bank balance will be at the end of the month. In this way a business will know what to expect and be able to make arrangements in advance, e.g. bank loan, overdraft, cut costs.
- Encourage cash not credit sales.
- Encourage early settlement of trade receivable accounts e.g. offer cash discounts for prompt payments, chase trade receivables regularly.
- Control overheads, e.g. rent, light, heat.
- Minimise drawings if sole trader or partnership; minimise dividends if an ltd or plc.
- Take advantage of cash discounts from trade payables to minimise the amounts you pay.

(ii) Liquid capital ratio

Formula

$$\text{Liquid capital ratio} = \frac{\text{Current assets - inventory}}{\text{Current liabilities}}$$

Meaning

It measures the immediate liquidity position of a business. It excludes inventory because it is the most difficult of the current assets to turn into cash. The ideal figure is about 1.

9.4 Gearing ratio

Formula

$$\text{Gearing ratio} = \frac{\text{Non-current liabilities}}{\text{Share capital + reserves + non - current liabilities}} \times 100$$

High gearing, low gearing and risk

High gearing is anything over 50%; low gearing is anything under 50%. Highly geared companies are considered risky because of two reasons:

- It increases the interest payments – therefore it means there is less profit available for dividends for the investors.
- It puts the firm at a bigger risk – because if it can't keep up with its loan repayments it might get liquidated.

9.5 Limitations of ratio analysis

Comparing like-with-like - differences in size, sector, age of the business and product mix make comparisons between companies very difficult.
Future plans - ratio analysis only looks at year-end figures. It doesn't tell us anything about what the company plans to do in the future e.g. launch new products, enter new markets or change CEO.
Non-financial factors - ratio analysis only looks at the numbers, it doesn't take into account non-financial factors such as location, quality of workers, quality of management, reputation of the company and brand loyalty.

General economic conditions – ratio analysis doesn't tell us anything about what has been happening in the economy. We may have a good set of figures because there has been a boom in the economy not because the company has performed well.

Inflation – a good set of figures could have been produced by high inflation not good performance

Window-dressing – firms can window-dress their accounts. This means deliberately flattering the accounts to make them look good, e.g. chasing-up trade receivables just before the year-end to bring the trade receivables period down; bringing forward sales to increase profits; using low rates of depreciation to increase profits.

Use of estimates - some of the figures in the accounts are based on estimates, e.g. depreciation, inventory valuation, provision for doubtful debts. Therefore the figures will never be 100% accurate.

9.6 The difference between profits and cash

Cash – cash is the physical amount of money a business has. Its cash receipts minus cash payments.

Profits – profits is revenue minus expenses. It takes into account sales where money hasn't been received yet and unpaid and prepaid expenses.

9.7 Summary of ratios

For a summary of ratio formulas see appendix 6.

Budgeting and budgetary control

10

10.1 Definition of a budget

A budget is a short-term financial plan. Usually they are prepared for a year in advance but some budgets are prepared over a month or per quarter.

10.2 Budgetary control

This means delegating financial planning to managers. Their performance is then evaluated against the budget and corrective action taken where necessary.

10.3 Types of budget

- Cash budget
- Sales budget
- Production budget
- Income statement budget
- Balance sheet budget
- Capital budget (non-current asset budget)
- Departmental budget

For the purposes of this unit you only need to know how to prepare a cash budget. See appendix 7 for layout.

10.4 Purposes/benefits of budgets

To set objectives/goals - budgets help businesses set goals and targets for the coming year. It helps them to focus on what they intend to achieve, e.g. profitability, productivity and market share
Planning - budgets help managers to plan ahead, e.g. raw materials and manpower requirements
Control - budgets provide a benchmark against which the actual figures can be measured. Variances can be investigated and corrective action taken, e.g. salaries too high - too much overtime being paid; interest payments too high - find alternative sources of finance.
Evaluation - budgets can be used to evaluate performance, e.g. sales staff and managers

Aids decision-making - budgets can help make better decisions, e.g. the cash budget can be used to see when the firm will be overdrawn and may need extra sources of finance.

Improves delegation – budgets help to divide up work into definite areas and give financial responsibilities to managers. This improves delegation.

Improves co-ordination & communication - as managers are clearer about their responsibilities it's easier to co-ordinate departments and communication improves.

Financial assets used more efficiently - budgets help managers allocate resources in the most efficient way, e.g. the cash budget helps to improve the management of working capital.

10.5 Drawbacks/limitations of budgets

De-motivation - targets can be set too high. Employees and managers may feel they can't achieve them and get de-motivated, e.g. sales budget.

Training – managers require training before they can use budgets. This may be costly.

Poorer decisions may be made – managers may stick to budgets too rigidly and therefore poorer decisions are made, e.g. a sales manager may refuse to increase spending on entertainment even though it might bring in more clients because he fears going over budget.

Loss of credibility – if there are lots of variances every year budgets may lose their credibility. Managers won't stick to them and complaints increase.

10.6 How the cash budget may benefit a business

The cash budget can benefit businesses in two ways:

- It can be used to identify when there will be a bank overdraft and therefore loan facilities can be arranged in advance.
- It can be used to motivate staff so that they don't overspend on expenses.

10.7 Cash budget layout

See Appendix 7.

Use of computers in accounting

11

11.1 Advantages/disadvantages

(i) Advantages

Speed - computers are much faster than manual systems because they use formulas and do adding up automatically.

Accuracy - computers are much more accurate than manual systems because again they use formulas. In this way casting errors are minimised.

Cuts down on storage requirements – this is because files and data are stored electronically. This means a firm can reduce their rental costs and it frees up office space to be used in another way.

Cuts costs - e.g. labour costs and storage costs. You need less people to do the work and it takes up less space.

Security - computers are more secure than manual systems because you can use passwords to control levels of access.

Management reports - computers can be used to produce reports and statistics which can be very useful to management, e.g. analysis of trade receivables, budgets, investment models, income statement, balance sheet.

Reduction in tedious work - computers reduce the amount of repetitive and boring tasks which need to be done. They can make work more interesting.

Makes work neater – work done on a computer is much easier to read and follow than work done by hand.

(ii) Disadvantages

Training - computers need well trained operators. This can be both costly and time consuming.

Security - computer systems may be less secure than manual ones. Passwords may be carelessly swapped by people and computers are open to hacking and fraud.

Systems support and documentation - user manuals and help desks may be inadequate or difficult to follow.

Cost - computers may be costly, particularly for small businessman.

11.2 Uses of computers in accounting

- Payrolls
- Inventory control
- Final accounts - income statement, balance sheet, statement of cash flows
- Forecasting & budgeting
- Decision making, e.g. break-even point, costing analysis
- Investment appraisal

11.3 Errors which a computer can and can't eliminate

Can

Errors of unequal amounts, e.g. transposition errors, brought forward errors and casting errors.

Can't

Errors of equal amounts, e.g. errors of omission, commission and principle.

11.4 Reasons why computerised inventory value may be lower than physical inventory value

- Transposition errors on input, e.g. 102 input for an item instead of 120
- Transcription errors on input, e.g. 52 input for an item instead of 55
- Errors of omission - items may have been completely missed out on input
- Goods returned not entered on computer system
- Software failure/hacking/virus
- Goods bought on sale or return haven't been entered on computer system

APPENDIX 1 – Income Statement Layout for Sole Traders

Income Statement for XYZ Co. for the year ended 31 December 20XX

	£	£
Revenue (revenue – returns in)		X
Cost of sales		
Opening inventory	X	
Add: Purchases	X	
(Purchases – returns out + carriage in)		
Less: Closing inventory	(X)	(X)
Gross profit		X
Discounts received		X
Rent received		X
Decrease in provision for doubtful debts		X
Bad debts recovered		X
Expenses		
Discount allowed	X	
Carriage out	X	
Rent	X	
Light & heat	X	
Insurance	X	
Wages	X	
General expenses	X	
Motor expenses	X	
Bad debts	X	
Interest paid	X	
Loss/gain on disposal	X/(X)	
Increase in provision for doubtful debts	X	
Depreciation	X	(X)
Profit for year		X

APPENDIX 2 – Balance Sheet Layout for Sole Traders

Balance sheet for XYZ Co. as at 31 December 20XX

	£ Cost	£ Depreciation	£ NBV
Non-current assets			
Premises	X	X	X
Plant & machinery	X	X	X
Motor vehicles	X	X	X
Fixtures & fittings	X	X	X
			X
Current assets			
Inventory		X	
Trade receivables		X	
Less: provision for doubtful debts		X	
Prepayments		X	
Bank		X	
Cash		X	X
Current liabilities			
Trade payables		X	
Accruals		X	
Bank overdraft		X	(X)
Net current assets			X
Non-current liabilities			
Bank loan		X	(X)
Net assets			X
Financed by			
Opening capital			X
Add: Profit for year			X
Less: Drawings			(X)
			X

APPENDIX 3 – Income Statement Layout for Ltd's

Income Statement for XYZ Ltd. for the year ended 31 December 20XX

	£	£
Revenue (revenue – returns in)		X
Cost of sales		
Opening inventory	X	
Add: Purchases	X	
(Purchases – returns out + carriage in)		
Less: Closing inventory	(X)	(X)
Gross profit		X
Discounts received		X
Rent received		X
Decrease in provision for doubtful debts		X
Bad debts recovered		X
Expenses		
Discount allowed	X	
Carriage out	X	
Rent	X	
Insurance	X	
Light & heat	X	
General expenses	X	
Motor expenses	X	
Bad debts	X	
Loss/gain on disposal	X/(X)	
Increase in provision for doubtful debts	X	
Depreciation	X	(X)
Profit from operations		X
Interest (finance costs)*		(X)
Profit for the year before tax		X
Taxation (income taxes)*		(X)
Profit for the year after taxes		X

*Finance costs and income taxes are the international terms. The examiner has stated that if they are used in Unit 2 then they will be shown together with the international term

APPENDIX 4 – Balance Sheet (Statement of Financial Position) Layout for Ltd's

Balance sheet for XYZ Ltd as at 31 December 20XX

Non-current assets	£ Cost	£ Depreciation	£ NBV
Premises	X	X	X
Plant & machinery	X	X	X
Motor vehicles	X	X	X
Fixtures & fittings	X	X	X
			X

Current assets			
Inventory		X	
Trade receivables		X	
Less: provision for doubtful debts		(X)	
Prepayments (other receivables)		X	
Cash and cash equivalents		X	X

Current liabilities			
Trade payables		X	
Accruals (other payables)		X	
Taxation		X	
Bank overdraft		X	(X)

Net current assets			X

Non-current liabilities			
Bank loan		X	
6% Debentures (2018-2020)		X	(X)

Net assets			X

Equity			
Ordinary shares £1 each			X
6% Preference shares £1 each			X
Share premium account			X
Revaluation reserve			X
General reserves			X
Retained earnings			X
			X

APPENDIX 5 – Statement of Changes in Equity

Statement of Changes in Equity for XYZ Ltd for the year ended 31 December 20XX

	Ordinary Shares £	Share Premium account £	Revaluation reserve £	Retained earnings £	Total £
At 1 Jan 20XX	X	X	X	X	X
Shares issued	X	X			X
Profit for year				X	X
Equity dividends*				(X)	X
Rev of property			X		
At 31 Dec 20XX	X	X	X	X	X

*Ordinary (equity) dividends paid only

APPENDIX 6 - Financial Ratios

(i) Performance ratios

$$ROCE = \frac{\text{Profit before tax \& interest (operating profit)}}{\text{Debentures} + \text{long term bank loans} + \text{share capital} + \text{reserves}} \times 100$$

$$\text{Gross Profit Margin} = \frac{\text{Gross profit}}{\text{Revenue}} \times 100$$

$$\text{Profit in relation to revenue} = \frac{\text{Profit for year}}{\text{Revenue}} \times 100$$

$$\text{Mark - up} = \frac{\text{Gross profit}}{\text{Cost of sales}} \times 100$$

$$\text{Overheads revenue percentage} = \frac{\text{Overheads}}{\text{Revenue}} \times 100$$

(ii) Activity ratios

$$\text{Inventory turnover} = \frac{\text{Cost of sales}}{\text{Average inventory}}$$

Or

$$\text{Inventory turnover} = \frac{\text{Average inventory}}{\text{Cost of sales}} \times 365 \text{ days}$$

$$\text{Receivable days} = \frac{\text{Trade receivables}}{\text{Credit sales}} \times 365 \text{ days}$$

$$\text{Payable days} = \frac{\text{Trade payables}}{\text{Credit purchases}} \times 365 \text{ days}$$

(iii) Liquidity

$$\text{Net current asset ratio} = \frac{\text{Current assets}}{\text{Current liabilities}}$$

$$\text{Liquid capital ratio} = \frac{\text{Current assets - inventory}}{\text{Current liabilities}}$$

(iv) Gearing

$$\text{Gearing ratio} = \frac{\text{Non-current liabilities}}{\text{Share capital + reserves + non - current liabilities}} \times 100$$

APPENDIX 7 – Cash Budget Layout

Receipts	J	F	M	A	M	J
	£	£	£	£	£	£
Cash sales	X	X	X	X	X	X
Credit sales		X	X	X	X	X
Rent received			X			X
	X	X	X	X	X	X
Payments						
Fixtures & fittings	X					
Motor vehicles	X					
Purchases	X	X	X	X	X	X
Rent			X			X
Light & heat	X	X	X	X	X	X
Insurance	X	X	X	X	X	X
Wages	X	X	X	X	X	X
Drawings	X	X	X	X	X	X
	(X)	(X)	(X)	(X)	(X)	(X)
Opening balance	X	X	X	X	X	X
Closing balance	X	X	X	X	X	X

APPENDIX 8 – Definitions of key terms

Non-current assets – these are assets which have a long-term function, can be used repeatedly, and were not bought for the purposes of resale, e.g. land & buildings, plant & machinery, motor vehicles. Another characteristic is that they depreciate.

Tangible non-current assets - these are non-current assets which you can see, touch and feel and which have a long-term function. They were bought for long term use by the business not for resale. They usually depreciate over their useful life, e.g. land & buildings, plant & machinery.

Intangible non-current assets - these are non-current assets which you can't see, touch and feel but have a long-term value to the business e.g. goodwill, patents, trademarks, copyrights.

Long-term investments - these are investments purchased for their profit earning capacity. They are usually in a similar or linked business and often have a strategic interest for the firm e.g. a firm may buy a controlling interest in a supplier. They are classified as non-current assets.

Short-term investments – these are investments in other companies which are held for profit from sale rather than for long-term earnings. They are likely to be held for less than one year and are classified as current assets. Please note that investments (short or long-term) are always stated at cost on the balance sheet. The market value is always shown in a note to the accounts.

Current assets - these are any assets owned by the business which are likely to be turned into cash before the next balance sheet date, usually within the year, e.g. inventory, trade receivables, cash.

Inventory - this is the unsold goods bought for resale to customers.

Trade receivables – this is the amount of money which customers owe the business.

Prepayments (other receivables) - these are expenses which have been paid in advance of the accounting period to which they relate.

Bank - this is the balance at the bank. If it's positive it will be shown as an asset, if it's negative it will be shown as a liability.

Current liabilities - these are liabilities owed by the firm which are likely to be paid in cash before the next balance sheet date, usually within one year, e.g. trade payables, accruals, bank overdraft.

Trade payables – this the amount of money the business owes to its suppliers.

Accruals (other payables) - these are the businesses unpaid expenses at the year end.

Proposed dividends - this is the unpaid dividends owed to shareholders at the year end.

Net current assets - this is current assets minus current liabilities. It's also known as working capital and is the finance available for the day-to-day running of the business.

Non-current liabilities - these are debts falling due after more than one year and include medium and long-term loans, e.g. debentures, bank loans.

Equity shareholders – this is another name for the ordinary shareholders in a limited company.

Equity capital - this is another name for the ordinary share capital of a business.

Operating profit - this means the profit on the businesses normal trading activities. It excludes extraordinary and exceptional items e.g. one-off profits on the sale of a property, one-off redundancy & factory closure costs.

Interim dividend - this is a dividend which is paid 6 months into the financial year.

Final dividend - this is the dividend which is paid at the end of the financial year.

Loan capital - this is the medium to long-term capital of a limited company provided either by banks or debenture holders.

Shareholders' funds - this is all of the share capital of the company plus all reserves. It includes both ordinary and preference shares.

Index